Language Lessons *for* Children

by Kathy Weitz

Primer One Spring

Student Book

Acknowledgements

Although my name is on the cover, the Primer series in many ways has been a collaborative effort. I owe a great debt of gratitude to many folks. The gorgeous cover designs are the craftsmanship of my friend Jayme Metzgar, with image credit to The Graphics Fairy (www.thegraphicsfairy.com). Many other friends have helped with both editing and content: in particular, Kimberlynn Curles, Emily Cook, Cheryl Turner, Karen Gill, Carolyn Vance, Lene Jaqua and the exceptional teachers, moms, and students of Providence Preparatory Academy. And of course, the main source of help and encouragement in myriad ways—from design consultation to field testing to dinner duty—has come from my dear husband and my wonderful children.

~kpw

Primer One Spring

Contents

The Swing

Writing Sentences
Homonyms
Making Plurals
Compound Words

from The Tale of Benjamin Bunny

Making Plural Possessive Forms
Making Plurals
Homonyms

from Proverbs

Making Contractions
Rhyming Words
Possessive Forms
Homonyms

from The Miracle

Similes
Spelling Rule: **y** *changing to* **i**
Possessive Forms
Homonyms
Rhyming Words

Psalm 23

Possessive Forms
Making Contractions
Similes
Homonyms

from My Country, 'Tis of Thee

Synonyms & Possessive Forms
Possessive Forms
Poem & Song Titles

from My Country, 'Tis of Thee

Rhyming Words
Possessive Forms
Antonyms

Weather Calendar
Plant Growth Chart

MATERIALS NEEDED FOR PRIMER ONE SPRING

All materials, resources, and links listed below are available at Cottage Press:

www.cottagepress.net

REQUIRED

- ❧ PRIMER ONE TEACHING HELPS ~ Required to effectively teach all lessons in in Primer. This one book contains teaching helps for all three Primer One student books. It contains instructions for all nature study and picture study lessons, tips and notes for teaching the Spelling, Grammar, and Word Usage lessons, and an answer key for the exercises that warrant it. Teach each lesson in Primer with this book open for ready reference.

- ❧ PRIMER RESOURCES WEBPAGE ~ Linked from *cottagepress.net* with many resources for nature and picture study. Bookmark this webpage.

- ❧ PICTURE STUDY PDFs ~ Free, downloadable PDFs for individual artists that include images of selected paintings along with biographical notes and links to many online resources. Available artists include: Audubon, Bruegel, Cassatt, DaVinci, Delacroix, Durer, Homer, Michelangelo, Millet, Monet, Rembrandt, Renoir, Rubens, Stuart, Titian, Van Eyck, Van Gogh, Vermeer. The *Primer Resources Webpage* has links to these free PDFs.

- ❧ THE ADVENTURES OF DANNY MEADOW MOUSE, BY THORNTON BURGESS ~ One in a series of delightful children's nature stories. Naturalist Thorton Burgess weaves accurate details about animal habits and characteristics into interesting and insightful storylines. All narration selections for *Primer One Spring* are found in this book. Purchase this from the Cottage Press bookstore or download it for free from Project Gutenberg as a PDF or ebook download.

  http://www.gutenberg.org/ebooks/25301

- ❧ A SYSTEMATIC PHONICS AND SPELLING PROGRAM ~ The lessons in the *Primer* books are designed to reinforce phonics and spelling rules taught in such a program. See recommendations on the *Primer Resources Webpage*.

OPTIONAL

- ❧ HIGH QUALITY COLORED PENCILS ~ Prismacolors by Berol are wonderful!

- ❧ BOOKS AND RESOURCES FOR THE NATURE AND PICTURE STUDY LESSONS ~ Links to resources (both free and for purchase) are available on the *Primer Resources Webpage*. Check your local library also.

WEEKLY LESSONS

THE SWING

How do you like to go up in a swing,

Up in the air so blue?

Oh, I do think it the pleasantest thing

Ever a child can do!

Up in the air and over the wall,

Till I can see so wide,

Rivers and trees and cattle and all

Over the countryside—

Till I look down on the garden green,

Down on the roof so brown

Up in the air I go flying again,

Up in the air and down!

~ Robert Louis Stevenson

Today is _____
                             Day   Date   Year

READ AND NARRATE

Danny Meadow Mouse Is Worried
~ *The Adventures of Danny Meadow Mouse* by Thornton W. Burgess

Vocabulary to study before you read:

grumpy	alone	uncomfortable
equally	miserable	homely
freckled	stout	elegantly
conscious	envious	moping

Draw a picture or series of pictures illustrating the story.

COPYBOOK

How do you like to go up in a swing,

Up in the air so blue?

Oh, I do think it the pleasantest thing

Ever a child can do!

_____

_____

_____

_____

WRITING SENTENCES

Write two sentences about things that are **blue.**

_____

_____

_____

HOMONYMS

Homonyms are words that sound alike but are spelled differently and have different meanings. **Blew** _is a homonym for_ **blue.** _Write one sentence using_ **blew.**

_____

_____

Today is _____

Day   Date   Year

NATURE STUDY

Plant some seeds this week. Follow the instructions in Teaching Helps. Draw and label the seeds in the first frame of the Plant Growth Chart in the Appendix.

Draw and label the parts of a flower in the box below.

COPYBOOK

Up in the air and over the wall,

Till I can see so wide,

Rivers and trees and cattle and all

Over the countryside—

_____

_____

_____

_____

_____

MAKING PLURALS

*We use the word **cow** when we want to talk about just one; we call this the **singular** form. We can use the word **cows** when we talk about two or more, but we might also use **cattle**; these are the **plural** forms. Many names of persons, places, or things are made plural by adding **-s** or **-es**, but there are times when the word changes completely, and some times when the word does not change at all.*

Write a sentence about more than one cow.

_____

Write a sentence about more than one mouse.

_____

Write a sentence about more than one sheep.

_____

Today is _____

Day   Date   Year

READ AND NARRATE

Danny Meadow Mouse and His Short Tail

~ *The Adventures of Danny Meadow Mouse* by Thornton W. Burgess

Vocabulary to study before you read:

ashamed	sulked	fidgeted
critically	twinkle	nuisance
satisfied	advice	

Draw a picture or series of pictures illustrating the story.

8

COPYBOOK

Till I look down on the garden green,

Down on the roof so brown

Up in the air I go flying again,

Up in the air and down!

_____

_____

_____

_____

_____

WRITING SENTENCES

Write two sentences about things that are green and two sentences about things that are brown.

_____

_____

_____

_____

_____

_____

Today is _____
                        Day   *Date*   *Year*

PICTURE STUDY

_____

_____

_____

In the space above, make your own rendering of the current work of art using colored pencils, or paste a printout from the Picture Study PDF. Write the title and date of the work on one line and the artist's name on the line below it.

Dictation

_____

_____

_____

_____

_____

_____

_____

_____

_____

Compound Words

Compound words are made by joining two whole words:

bird + house = birdhouse   earth + worm = earthworm

Find the compound word in this week's selection and use it in a sentence. Think of two more compound words and write them on the lines below your sentence.

_____

_____

_____

from THE TALE OF BENJAMIN BUNNY

They went away hand in hand, and got upon the flat top of the wall at the bottom of the wood. From here they looked down into Mr. McGregor's garden. Peter's shoes and coat were plainly to be seen upon the scarecrow, topped with an old tam-o-shanter of Mr. McGregor's.

Little Benjamin said, "It spoils people's clothes to squeeze under a gate; the proper way to get in, is to climb down a pear tree."

Peter fell down head first; but it was of no consequence, as the bed below was newly raked and quite soft.

It had been sown with lettuces.

They left a great many odd little foot-marks all over the bed, especially little Benjamin, who was wearing clogs.

~ Beatrix Potter

Today is _____
                          Day   Date   Year

READ AND NARRATE

Danny Meadow Mouse Plays Hide and Seek
~ The Adventures of Danny Meadow Mouse by Thornton W. Burgess

Vocabulary to study before you read:

furry-coated	feathers	stout-hearted
snowflakes	tunnels	footprints
tiptoeing	frantic	scurrying

Draw a picture or series of pictures illustrating the story.

COPYBOOK

They went away hand in hand, and got upon the flat top of the wall at the bottom of the wood. From here they looked down into Mr. McGregor's garden. Peter's shoes and coat were plainly to be seen upon the scarecrow, topped with an old tam-o-shanter of Mr. McGregor's.

_____

_____

_____

_____

_____

MAKING PLURAL POSSESSIVE FORMS

*An **apostrophe** (') + s is added to a word to show ownership.*

John's hat = the hat belonging to John

Two names in today's selection are possessive. Write them below (one name is used as a possessive twice - only write it once).

_____

_____

Write one sentence below using a possessive from the selection. Include the thing possessed.

Example: Peter's shoes were on the scarecrow.

_____

_____

Write the compound word from today's selection. _____

Today is

_____

| Day | Date | Year |

NATURE STUDY

Choose a plant and talk about its characteristics, covering the points below. Then, sketch the plant in the frame on the left below. Write its name on the line.

❑ Its size

❑ Its season

❑ Its culture - seed, bulb, or cutting?

❑ Its roots, stem, leaves, flower, fruit, and seeds

❑ Its uses

Draw your growing plants on the Plant Growth Chart in the Appendix.

COPYBOOK
_____

Little Benjamin said, "It spoils people's clothes to squeeze under a gate; the proper way to get in, is to climb down a pear tree."

Peter fell down head first; but it was of no consequence, as the bed below was newly raked and quite soft.

_____

_____

_____

_____

_____

_____

MAKING PLURALS
_____

*To make a word that names a person, place, thing, or idea plural we usually add **-s** or **-es** to it. Some words change internally or completely when they become plural. Write the plural forms on the line below each of the following words.*

person   shoe   church

_____

tooth   gate   watch

_____

man   tree   fish

_____

17

Today is _____

READ AND NARRATE

Old Granny Fox Tries for Danny Meadow Mouse

~ The Adventures of Danny Meadow Mouse by Thornton W. Burgess

Vocabulary to study before you read:

caught	dangerous	disgust
muttering	heart	exciting
sniffed	ducked	plunged
squeaked		

Draw a picture or series of pictures illustrating the story.

COPYBOOK

It had been sown with lettuces.

They left a great many odd little foot-marks all over the bed, especially little Benjamin, who was wearing clogs.

_____

_____

_____

_____

_____

MAKING PLURAL POSSESSIVE FORMS

Form the possessive by adding an **apostrophe (')** + **s.**

Peter's shoes; people's clothes

To form the possessive of plural words ending in **-s,** *add the* **apostrophe (')** *alone:*

bunnies' shoes; birds' nests

Write the correct possessive forms below.

coats of rabbits   _____

walls of gardens   _____

honey of bees   _____

chirp of crickets   _____

wings of birds   _____

Today is

_____

Day   Date   Year

PICTURE STUDY
_____

_____

_____

_____

Dictation

_____

_____

_____

_____

_____

Homonyms

Homonyms sound alike but are spelled differently and have different meanings. **Sown** _is a homonym for_ **sewn**. _Write one sentence using_ **sewn**.

_____

_____

Here are a few more words that have homonyns. Write a homonym for each on the line following it. Some of the words have more than one.

shoe _____

way _____

sew _____

rows _____

eye _____

ate _____

from PROVERBS

My son, do not forget my law,

    but let your heart keep my commands;

    for length of days and long life

    and peace they will add to you.

Let not mercy and truth forsake you;

    bind them around your neck,

    write them on the tablet of your heart,

    and so find favor and high esteem

    in the sight of God and man.

Trust in the Lord with all your heart,

    and lean not on your own understanding;

    in all your ways acknowledge Him,

    and He shall direct your paths.

~ Proverbs 3:1-6, New King James Version

Today is _____
                           Day   *Date*   *Year*

READ AND NARRATE

What Happened on the Green Meadows
~ *The Adventures of Danny Meadow Mouse* by Thornton W. Burgess

Vocabulary to study before you read:

regular	immensely	listened
keen	selfish	temper
noise	scratched	

Draw a picture or series of pictures illustrating the story.

COPYBOOK

My son, do not forget my law,

but let your heart keep my commands;

for length of days and long life

and peace they will add to you.

_____

_____

_____

_____

MAKING CONTRACTIONS

A contraction shortens a group of words by replacing a letter or letters with an **apostrophe (').**

do not = don't

Write the contraction for each group of words below.

let us _____

they will _____

He shall _____

have not _____

you are _____

Today is _____
  Day   Date   Year

NATURE STUDY

Choose a plant and talk about its characteristics, covering the points below. Then, sketch the plant in the frame on the left below. Write its name on the line.

    ❑ Its size

    ❑ Its season

    ❑ Its culture - seed, bulb, or cutting?

    ❑ Its roots, stem, leaves, flower, fruit, and seeds

    ❑ Its uses

Draw your growing plants on the Plant Growth Chart in the Appendix.

COPYBOOK

Let not mercy and truth forsake you;

    bind them around your neck,

    write them on the tablet of your heart,

    and so find favor and high esteem

    in the sight of God and man.

RHYMING WORDS

Write three words that rhyme with **heart.**

Write three words that rhyme with **write.**

Write three words that rhyme with **bind.**

Today is _____

Read And Narrate

Danny Meadow Mouse Remembers and Reddy Fox Forgets
~ *The Adventures of Danny Meadow Mouse* by Thornton W. Burgess

Vocabulary to study before you read:

spry	smarted	crashed
hollow	barbs	excited
dreadfully	hobbled	

Draw a picture or series of pictures illustrating the story.

COPYBOOK

Trust in the Lord with all your heart,

and lean not on your own understanding;

in all your ways acknowledge Him,

and He shall direct your paths.

POSSESSIVE FORMS

Some words are possessive all on their own and do not need an added **'s.**

my, our, your, his, her, its, their

Write each of the following pronouns with an appropriate thing owned; for example, **my = my neck.**

your _____

our _____

his _____

its _____

their _____

Today is _____

Day   *Date*   *Year*

PICTURE STUDY

_____

_____

_____

DICTATION

_____

_____

_____

_____

_____

_____

_____

_____

HOMONYMS

Some possessive words are homonyms for contractions. **Your** _is possessive;_ **you're** _is the contraction for_ **you are.** _Write two sentences below. Use_ **your** _in one and_ **you're** _in the other. Take care to use the correct form in your writing._

_____

_____

_____

_____

from THE MIRACLE

The next day was foggy. Everything on the farm was dripping wet. The grass looked like a magic carpet. The asparagus patch looked like a silver forest.

On foggy mornings, Charlotte's web was truly a thing of beauty. This morning each thin strand was decorated with dozens of tiny beads of water. The web glistened in the light and made a pattern of loveliness and mystery, like a delicate veil. Even Lurvy, who wasn't particularly interested in beauty, noticed the web when he came with the pig's breakfast. He noted how clearly it showed up and he noted how big and carefully built it was. And then he took another look and he saw something that made him set his pail down.

~ *Charlotte's Web*, by E.B. White

Today is _____

Read And Narrate

Old Granny Fox Tries a New Plan

~ The Adventures of Danny Meadow Mouse by Thornton W. Burgess

Vocabulary to study before you read:

snug	danger	forbade
grumbled	mumbled	disobey
hidden	limped	stretched

Draw a picture or series of pictures illustrating the story.

COPYBOOK
_____

The next day was foggy. Everything on the farm was dripping wet. The grass looked like a magic carpet. The asparagus patch looked like a silver forest.

_____
_____
_____
_____
_____

SIMILES
_____

A simile compares two things that are not usually associated with one another by using the words **like**, **as**, *or* **than**.

Her smile was like sunshine.

In this example, her smile *is being compared to* sunshine.

Find two similes in today's copybook selection. What is being compared in each?

_____
is compared to

_____
is compared to

Authors will often use similes when they wants you to imagine what they are describing—to actually see a picture in your mind. Look and listen for similes in your reading this week. Write them below.

_____
_____

35

Today is _____

Day   Date   Year

NATURE STUDY

Choose a plant and talk about its characteristics, covering the points below. Then, sketch the plant in the frame on the left below. Write its name on the line.

❑ Its size

❑ Its season

❑ Its culture - seed, bulb, or cutting?

❑ Its roots, stem, leaves, flower, fruit, and seeds

❑ Its uses

_____

Draw your growing plants on the Plant Growth Chart in the Appendix.

COPYBOOK

On foggy mornings, Charlotte's web was truly a thing of beauty. This morning each thin strand was decorated with dozens of tiny beads of water. The web glistened in the light and made a pattern of loveliness and mystery, like a delicate veil.

SPELLING RULE: Y CHANGING TO I

Y *is sometimes used as a vowel, saying /ĭ/, /ī/, or /ē/. Words that end with the single vowel -y usually exchange the y for an i when we add a suffix to the word, unless the suffix begins with an i-.*

try + ed → tried   try + ing → trying

Add the suffix to the root word below, following the y changing to i rule.

lovely + ness   beauty + full   foggy + er

cry + ing   early + er   joy + full

37

Today is _____
Day   Date   Year

READ AND NARRATE

Brother North Wind Proves a Friend
~ The Adventures of Danny Meadow Mouse by Thornton W. Burgess

Vocabulary to study before you read:

tomorrow	forgotten	wee
forgotten	heaped	shook
snarl	disappointment	

Draw a picture or series of pictures illustrating the story.

COPYBOOK

Even Lurvy, who wasn't particularly interested in beauty, noticed the web when he came with the pig's breakfast. He noted how clearly it showed up and he noted how big and carefully built it was. And then he took another look and he saw something that made him set his pail down.

_____

_____

_____

_____

_____

_____

POSSESSIVE FORMS

Write the correct possessive forms below.

beauty of the web   _____

web of Charlotte   _____

breakfast of pigs   _____

pail of Lurvy   _____

SIMILES

Find a simile in yesterday's copybook selection. What two things are being compared?

_____ is compared to _____

Today is _____

Day   Date   Year

PICTURE STUDY

_____

_____

_____

DICTATION

_____

_____

_____

_____

_____

_____

HOMONYMS

The homonym of **veil** *is* **vale**. *If you do not know what a* **vale** *is, ask your teacher to help you look it up in the dictionary. Write its meaning below.*

_____

Write homonyms for the following words.

pail   _____

our   _____

RHYMING WORDS

Write three words that rhyme with **veil**.

_____

Write three words that rhyme with **bead**.

_____

41

Psalm 23

The Lord is my shepherd;
   I shall not want.
He makes me to lie down in green pastures;
   He leads me beside the still waters.
He restores my soul;
   He leads me in the paths of righteousness
   For His name's sake.

Yea, though I walk through the valley of the shadow of death,
   I will fear no evil;
   For You are with me;
   Your rod and Your staff, they comfort me.

You prepare a table before me in the presence of my enemies;
   You anoint my head with oil;
   My cup runs over.
Surely goodness and mercy shall follow me
   All the days of my life;
   And I will dwell in the house of the Lord
   Forever.

~ New King James Version

Today is _____
               Day   *Date*   *Year*

READ AND NARRATE

Danny Meadow Mouse Is Caught At Last
~ *The Adventures of Danny Meadow Mouse* by Thornton W. Burgess

Vocabulary to study before you read:

happiness	smarter	disgust
dodged	forgot	forgetting
frolic	drifts	floated

Draw a picture or series of pictures illustrating the story.

COPYBOOK

The Lord is my shepherd;

    I shall not want.

He makes me to lie down in green pastures;

    He leads me beside the still waters.

He restores my soul;

    He leads me in the paths of righteousness

    For His name's sake.

_____

_____

_____

_____

_____

_____

POSSESSIVE FORMS

Write the alternate possessive forms.

paths of righteousness   _____

His name's sake   _____

Today is _____

NATURE STUDY

Choose a plant and talk about its characteristics, covering the points below. Then, sketch the plant in the frame on the left below. Write its name on the line.

- ❑ Its size
- ❑ Its season
- ❑ Its culture - seed, bulb, or cutting?
- ❑ Its roots, stem, leaves, flower, fruit, and seeds
- ❑ Its uses

Draw your growing plants on the Plant Growth Chart in the Appendix.

COPYBOOK

Yea, though I walk through the valley of the shadow of death,

I will fear no evil;

For You are with me;

Your rod and Your staff, they comfort me.

_____

_____

_____

_____

_____

MAKING CONTRACTIONS

Write the contraction for each of the phrases.

I shall   _____

I will   _____

he is   _____

there is   _____

she had   _____

Today is _____

READ AND NARRATE

A Strange Ride and How It Ended
~ The Adventures of Danny Meadow Mouse by Thornton W. Burgess

Vocabulary to study before you read:

speck	wonderful	terrible
beautiful	moonlight	wriggle
struggle	squirmed	twisted

Draw a picture or series of pictures illustrating the story.

COPYBOOK

You prepare a table before me in the presence of my enemies;
    You anoint my head with oil;
    My cup runs over.
Surely goodness and mercy shall follow me
    All the days of my life;
    And I will dwell in the house of the Lord
    Forever.

_____

_____

_____

_____

_____

_____

_____

_____

SIMILES

Think of a simile using the word **like** *to compare the Lord with a shepherd. Write a sentence using your simile.*

_____

_____

Today is _____

                              Day   *Date*   *Year*

PICTURE STUDY

Dictation

_____

_____

'

_____

_____

_____

_____

_____

_____

Homonyms

Write a homonym for this word.

through _____

Write two sentences, one for the original word, and one for its homonym. Take care to use the correct form in your writing.

_____

_____

_____

THE FLOWERS

All the names I know from nurse:
Gardener's garters, Shepherd's purse,
Bachelor's buttons, Lady smock,
And the Lady Hollyhock.

Fairy places, fairy things,
Fairy woods where the wild bee wings,
Tiny trees for tiny dames –
These must all be fairy names!

Tiny woods below whose boughs
Shady fairies weave a house;
Tiny tree-tops, rose or thyme,
Where the braver fairies climb!

Fair are grown-up people's trees
But the fairest woods are these;
Where, if I were not so tall,
I should live for good and all.

~ Robert Louis Stevenson

Today is _____

READ AND NARRATE

Peter Rabbit Gets a Fright

~ The Adventures of Danny Meadow Mouse by Thornton W. Burgess

Vocabulary to study before you read:

decide	travels	dull
interest	neighborly	cheeriest
orchard	somersault	insects

Draw a picture or series of pictures illustrating the story.

COPYBOOK

All the names I know from nurse:

Gardener's garters, Shepherd's purse,

Bachelor's buttons, Lady smock,

And the Lady Hollyhock.

_____

_____

_____

_____

_____

PHONOGRAM CK

The sound /k/ can be spelled with the two-letter phonogram ck, but only after a short vowel. The phonogram ck is never used at the beginning of a word, after long vowels, or after vowel teams. Copy the words with the phonogram ck below.

smock	hollyhock	checkers
wick	buckle	sticky
prick	unlock	hickory

Today is _____
                     Day   *Date*   *Year*

NATURE STUDY

Read about cloud types with your teacher (see Teacher Helps). Draw and label the following kinds of clouds in the boxes below.

Cirrus

Stratus

Cumulus

Cumulonimbus

Begin to keep track of the weather every day this month on the calendar provided in the Appendix.

Fairy places, fairy things,

Fairy woods where the wild bee wings,

Tiny trees for tiny dames —

These must all be fairy names!

Tiny woods below whose boughs

Shady fairies weave a house;

Tiny tree-tops, rose or thyme,

Where the braver fairies climb!

_____

_____

_____

_____

_____

_____

_____

_____

Today is _____

Day	Date	Year

READ AND NARRATE
_____

The Old Briar-Patch Has a New Tenant

~ The Adventures of Danny Meadow Mouse by Thornton W. Burgess

Vocabulary to study before you read:

pleasant	voice	knocked
breath	comfortable	brambles
lonesome	gratefully	tenant

Draw a picture or series of pictures illustrating the story.

COPYBOOK

Fair are grown-up people's trees

But the fairest woods are these;

Where, if I were not so tall,

I should live for good and all.

_____

_____

_____

_____

_____

HOMONYMS

Write a homonym for each word.

I   _____

know   _____

fair   _____

bee   _____

boughs   _____

thyme   _____

for   _____

59

Today is _____
Day   Date   Year

Picture Study

_____

_____

_____

Dictation

Possessive Forms

Write the possessive forms from this week's selection, and then write the alternate form next to it.

Examples: **baby's breath** **breath of baby**

from Pooh Invents a New Game and Eeyore Joins In

By the time it came to the edge of the Forest, the stream had grown up, so that it was almost a river, and being grown-up, it did not run and jump and sparkle along as it used to do when it was younger, but moved more slowly. For it knew now where it was going, and it said to itself, "There is no hurry. We shall get there someday." But all the little streams higher up in the Forest went this way and that, quickly, eagerly, having so much to find out before it was too late.

There was a broad track, almost as broad as a road, leading from the Outland to the Forest, but before it could come to the Forest, it had to cross this river. So, where it crossed, there was a wooden bridge, almost as broad as a road, with wooden rails on each side of it.

~ *The House at Pooh Corner,* by A.A. Milne

Today is _____

READ AND NARRATE

Peter Rabbit Visits the Peach Orchard
~ *The Adventures of Danny Meadow Mouse* by Thornton W. Burgess

Vocabulary to study before you read:

moonlit	disapproval	content
present	nibbled	stripping
sap	impossible	stomach

Draw a picture or series of pictures illustrating the story.

COPYBOOK

By the time it came to the edge of the Forest, the stream had grown up, so that it was almost a river, and being grown-up, it did not run and jump and sparkle along as it used to do when it was younger, but moved more slowly.

WRITING BOOK TITLES

When you handwrite the title of a book, you should capitalize the first word and every important word in the title. Underline book titles, but not the author of the book.

<u>The Wind in the Willows</u>, by Kenneth Grahame

Write the titles and authors of four books you have read.

Today is _____

Day   Date   Year

Nature Study

With your teacher, study the water cycle (see Teaching Helps). In the frame below, draw and label the water cycle. Include: evaporation, condensation, precipitation, accumulation (collection).

Remember to make notes on your weather calendar every day this month.

COPYBOOK

For it knew now where it was going, and it said to itself, "There is no hurry. We shall get there someday." But all the little streams higher up in the Forest went this way and that, quickly, eagerly, having so much to find out before it was too late.

_____

_____

_____

_____

_____

COULD, SHOULD, WOULD

In these words, the phonogram **ou** *says* /**oo**/ *like in* **book**. *The* **l** *is silent.*

Write contractions with could, would, *and* should.

would + not   _____

could + not   _____

should + not   _____

Write a sentence using one of the contractions you made.

_____

_____

Today is _____

READ AND NARRATE

Farmer Brown Sets a Trap
~ The Adventures of Danny Meadow Mouse by Thornton W. Burgess

Vocabulary to study before you read:

mischief	dared	curious
cautiously	crept	wrapped
wire	netting	tugged

Draw a picture or series of pictures illustrating the story.

Copybook

There was a broad track, almost as broad as a road, leading from the Outland to the Forest, but before it could come to the Forest, it had to cross this river. So, where it crossed, there was a wooden bridge, almost as broad as a road, with wooden rails on each side of it.

_____

_____

_____

_____

_____

_____

Writing Chapter Titles

When you handwrite the title of a chapter, you should capitalize the first word and every important word in the title. Chapter titles should be enclosed in quotes.

"Pooh Invents a New Game"

Write the titles of three or four chapters from The Adventures of Danny Meadow Mouse *by Thornton Burgess. Use quotation marks.*

_____

_____

_____

_____

Today is _____

Day   Date   Year

PICTURE STUDY

DICTATION

_____

_____

_____

_____

_____

_____

_____

HOMONYMS

Here are a few more words that have homonyns. Write a homonym for each. Some of these words have more than one homonym, so write as many as you can.

to _____

by _____

knew _____

high _____

so _____

road _____

wood _____

from THE CICADA

The Common Cicada likes to lay her eggs on small dry branches. She chooses, as far as possible, tiny stalks, which may be of any size between that of a straw and a lead-pencil. The sprig is never lying on the ground, is usually nearly upright in position, and is almost always dead.

Having found a twig to suit her, she makes a row of pricks with the sharp instrument on her chest — such pricks as might be made with a pin if it were driven downwards on a slant, so as to tear the fibres and force them slightly upwards. If she is undisturbed she will make thirty or forty of these pricks on the same twig.

In the tiny cells formed by these pricks she lays her eggs. The cells are narrow passages, each one slanting down towards the one below it. I generally find about ten eggs in each cell, so it is plain that the Cicada lays between three and four hundred eggs altogether.

~ *Fabre's Book of Insects*, by Jean-Henri Fabre

Today is _____

            Day   Date   Year

READ AND NARRATE

Peter Rabbit Is Caught in a Snare
~ The Adventures of Danny Meadow Mouse by Thornton W. Burgess

Vocabulary to study before you read:

startled	tightened	stake
snare	fastened	hope
pitched	disappointment	

Draw a picture or series of pictures illustrating the story.

Copybook

The Common Cicada likes to lay her eggs on small dry branches. She chooses, as far as possible, tiny stalks, which may be of any size between that of a straw and a lead-pencil. The sprig is never lying on the ground, is usually nearly upright in position, and is almost always dead.

Writing Sentences

Complete this sentence with the chapter name and the book title from which this week's copybook selection is taken. Use the correct form for writing a book title and mention the name of the author. If you have room, add a sentence telling something you learned from the copybook selection.

Today's copybook selection is taken from

Today is _____
            Day   Date   Year

NATURE STUDY

Discuss these characteristics of insects:

- ✓ do not have a backbone, but have an exoskeleton
- ✓ have three main body parts: head, thorax, and abdomen
- ✓ have a pair of antennae on their head
- ✓ have three pairs of legs
- ✓ have two pairs of wings

List 5 kinds of insects below.

1. _____

2. _____

3. _____

4. _____

5. _____

In the frame below, draw an insect. Label the following parts: head, thorax, abdomen, antennae, wings, legs.

Remember to make notes on your weather calendar every day this month.

COPYBOOK

Having found a twig to suit her, she makes a row of pricks with the sharp instrument on her chest — such pricks as might be made with a pin if it were driven downwards on a slant, so as to tear the fibres and force them slightly upwards. If she is undisturbed she will make thirty or forty of these pricks on the same twig.

RHYMING WORDS

Write three words that rhyme with **twig**.

Write three words that rhyme with **chest**.

Write three words that rhyme with **slant**.

Today is

<table>
<tr><td>Day</td><td>Date</td><td>Year</td></tr>
</table>

READ AND NARRATE

Peter Rabbit's Hard Journey

~ The Adventures of Danny Meadow Mouse by Thornton W. Burgess

Vocabulary to study before you read:

<table>
<tr><td>safest</td><td>waiting</td><td>drawn</td></tr>
<tr><td>fastened</td><td>stiff</td><td>heavier</td></tr>
<tr><td>dreadful</td><td>content</td><td>anxiously</td></tr>
</table>

Draw a picture or series of pictures illustrating the story.

COPYBOOK
_____

    In the tiny cells formed by these pricks she lays her eggs. The cells are narrow passages, each one slanting down towards the one below it. I generally find about ten eggs in each cell, so it is plain that the Cicada lays between three and four hundred eggs altogether.

_____

_____

_____

_____

_____

_____

WRITING NUMBERS
_____

Write the words that express these numbers.

hundred	thousand	million

_____

500   _____

8,000   _____

2,000,000   _____

Today is _____
                       Day   *Date*   *Year*

PICTURE STUDY

DICTATION

_____

_____

_____

_____

_____

_____

ANTONYMS

Antonyms are words that have opposite meanings, like **happy** and **sad**. Beside each word below write one or more antonyms.

dry _____

tiny _____

sharp _____

dead _____

ground _____

down _____

near _____

narrow _____

THE WORM

When the earth is turned in spring
The worms are fat as anything.

And birds come flying all around
To eat the worms right off the ground.

They like worms just as much as I
Like bread and milk and apple pie.

And once, when I was very young,
I put a worm right on my tongue.

I didn't like the taste a bit,
And so I didn't swallow it.

But oh, it makes my mother squirm
Because she thinks I ate that worm!

~ by Ralph Bergengren

Today is _____

                  Day   *Date*   *Year*

Read And Narrate

Danny Meadow Mouse Becomes Worried
~ *The Adventures of Danny Meadow Mouse* by Thornton W. Burgess

Vocabulary to study before you read:

limped	lame	sore
kindness	brought	worrying
crawling	caught	snare

Draw a picture or series of pictures illustrating the story.

Copybook

When the earth is turned in spring

The worms are fat as anything.

And birds come flying all around

To eat the worms right off the ground.

_____

_____

_____

_____

_____

Spellings of /er/

The sound /er/ is made by **er** (as in her), **ir** (as in first), **ur** (as in church), **ear** (as in early), and **or** used after **w** (as in worship). Read and copy these words which have the /er/ sound.

earth	worms	birds
squirm	spur	winter
world	every	early

Today is _____
                    Day   Date   Year

NATURE STUDY

Choose an insect and talk about its characteristics, covering the points below. Sketch the insect in the frame. Write the name of the insect on the line below the frame.

- ❏ Its size
- ❏ Its life cycle
- ❏ Its food
- ❏ Its means of protecting itself
- ❏ Its habits

Remember to make notes on your weather calendar every day this month.

COPYBOOK

They like worms just as much as I

Like bread and milk and apple pie.

And once, when I was very young,

I put a worm right on my tongue.

_____

_____

_____

_____

_____

CONTRACTIONS

Write the contraction for each of these phrases.

did not   _____

have not   _____

is not   _____

do not   _____

will not*   _____

*The contraction for will not *is tricky. Change the letters* **ill** *to* **o**.

Today is _____
                    Day   Date   Year

READ AND NARRATE

Danny Meadow Mouse Returns a Kindness
~ *The Adventures of Danny Meadow Mouse* by Thornton W. Burgess

Vocabulary to study before you read:

lay	wit	spry
twitches	gnaw	splinters
bothersome	secretest	retreat

Draw a picture or series of pictures illustrating the story.

COPYBOOK

I didn't like the taste a bit,

And so I didn't swallow it.

But oh, it makes my mother squirm

Because she thinks I ate that worm!

_____

_____

_____

_____

_____

POSSESSIVE FORMS

Write the alternate possessive form.

tongue of me   _____

mother of me   _____

beaks of birds   _____

apple pie of you   _____

bread of her   _____

bodies of worms   _____

Today is

_____

| Day | Date | Year |

Picture Study

_____

_____

_____

_____

DICTATION

_____

_____

_____

_____

_____

_____

_____

_____

SYNONYMS

Synonyms are words that have similar meanings, like **happy** _and_ **glad**. _Beside each word below write one or more synonyms._

earth _____

fat _____

young _____

sky _____

chirping _____

small _____

big _____

from HOW THE RHINOCEROS GOT HIS SKIN

And the Rhinoceros did. He buttoned it up with the three buttons, and it tickled like cake crumbs in bed. Then he wanted to scratch, but that made it worse; and then he lay down on the sands and rolled and rolled and rolled, and every time he rolled the cake crumbs tickled him worse and worse and worse. Then he ran to the palm-tree and rubbed and rubbed and rubbed himself against it. He rubbed so much and so hard that he rubbed his skin into a great fold over his shoulders, and another fold underneath, where the buttons used to be (but he rubbed the buttons off), and he rubbed some more folds over his legs. And it spoiled his temper, but it didn't make the least difference to the cake-crumbs. They were inside his skin and they tickled. So he went home, very angry indeed and horribly scratchy; and from that day to this every rhinoceros has great folds in his skin and a very bad temper, all on account of the cake-crumbs inside.

~ *Just So Stories*, by Rudyard Kipling

Today is _____

Day   Date   Year

READ AND NARRATE

Peter Rabbit and Danny Meadow Mouse Live High
~ The Adventures of Danny Meadow Mouse by Thornton W. Burgess

Vocabulary to study before you read:

swelled	curious	studied
queer	suffered	tight
miserable	steal	bait

Draw a picture or series of pictures illustrating the story.

COPYBOOK

And the Rhinoceros did. He buttoned it up with the three buttons, and it tickled like cake crumbs in bed. Then he wanted to scratch, but that made it worse; and then he lay down on the sands and rolled and rolled and rolled, and every time he rolled the cake crumbs tickled him worse and worse and worse. Then he ran to the palm-tree and rubbed and rubbed and rubbed himself against it.

_____

_____

_____

_____

_____

_____

_____

_____

SIMILES

Find the simile in today's copybook selection. What two things are being compared? (Hint: Remember to look for the word like._)_

_____   is compared to   _____

Today is _____

                    Day   Date   Year

NATURE STUDY

Choose an insect and talk about its characteristics, covering the points below. Sketch the insect in the frame. Write the name of the insect on the line below the frame.

- ❑ Its size
- ❑ Its life cycle
- ❑ Its food
- ❑ Its means of protecting itself
- ❑ Its habits

Remember to make notes on your weather calendar every day this month.

COPYBOOK
_____

He rubbed so much and so hard that he rubbed his skin into a great fold over his shoulders, and another fold underneath, where the buttons used to be (but he rubbed the buttons off), and he rubbed some more folds over his legs. And it spoiled his temper, but it didn't make the least difference to the cake-crumbs.

_____

_____

_____

_____

_____

_____

SYNONYMS
_____

Find and write the synonyms from today's copybook selection for each of these words.

scratched   _____

roughly   _____

huge   _____

ruined   _____

attitude   _____

Today is _____

READ AND NARRATE

Timid Danny Meadow Mouse
~ The Adventures of Danny Meadow Mouse by Thornton W. Burgess

Vocabulary to study before you read:

timid   certainly   homely

innocent   foolish   guard

queerly   admit

Draw a picture or series of pictures illustrating the story.

COPYBOOK

They were inside his skin and they tickled. So he went home, very angry indeed and horribly scratchy; and from that day to this every rhinoceros has great folds in his skin and a very bad temper, all on account of the cake-crumbs inside.

_____

_____

_____

_____

_____

_____

ANTONYMS

Write antonyms for each of these words from this week's copybook selection.

up _____

hard _(as it is used in the selection)_ _____

great _(as it is used in the selection)_ _____

over _____

bad _(as it is used in the selection)_ _____

love _____

hot _____

inside _____

Today is _____

Day　　　　　　　　　　Date　　　　　　　　　　Year

PICTURE STUDY _____

_____

_____

_____

Dictation

_____

_____

_____

_____

_____

_____

_____

_____

Rhyming Words

Write three words that rhyme with **scratch.**

_____

Write three words that rhyme with **more.**

_____

Write three words that rhyme with **least.**

_____

Write three words that rhyme with **very.**

_____

from MY COUNTRY, 'TIS OF THEE

My country, 'tis of thee,

Sweet land of liberty,

Of thee I sing;

Land where my fathers died,

Land of the Pilgrims' pride,

From every mountainside

Let freedom ring.

My native country, thee,

Land of the noble free—

Thy name I love;

I love thy rocks and rills,

Thy woods and templed hills;

My heart with rapture thrills

Like that above.

~ Samuel Francis Smith

Today is _____

Day   Date   Year

READ AND NARRATE

An Exciting Day for Danny Meadow Mouse
~ The Adventures of Danny Meadow Mouse by Thornton W. Burgess

Vocabulary to study before you read:

exciting	working	private
rusting	wits	knot-hole
disappear	fool	scampered

Draw a picture or series of pictures illustrating the story.

Copybook

My country, 'tis of thee,

Sweet land of liberty,

Of thee I sing;

Land where my fathers died,

Land of the Pilgrims' pride,

From every mountainside

Let freedom ring.

_____

_____

_____

_____

_____

_____

_____

Synonyms & Possessive Forms

Find both pairs of synonyms in today's selection. Write one pair below.

_____

Find the possessive form which uses an apostrophe in today's selection and write it along with its alternate form. (**John's hat = hat of John**)

_____

Today is _____
            Day   Date   Year

NATURE STUDY

Choose an insect and talk about its characteristics, covering the points below. Sketch the insect in the frame. Write the name of the insect on the line below the frame.

- ❑ Its size
- ❑ Its life cycle
- ❑ Its food
- ❑ Its means of protecting itself
- ❑ Its habits

Remember to make notes on your weather calendar every day this month.

COPYBOOK

My native country, thee,

Land of the noble free—

    Thy name I love;

I love thy rocks and rills,

Thy woods and templed hills;

My heart with rapture thrills

    Like that above.

___

___

___

___

___

___

___

POSSESSIVE FORMS

Find the possessive forms which do not use an apostrophe in today's selection and write them along with the thing possessed.

___

___

Today is _____

READ AND NARRATE _____

What Happened Next to Danny Meadow Mouse
~ The Adventures of Danny Meadow Mouse by Thornton W. Burgess

Vocabulary to study before you read:

escapes   cautiously   keen

satisfied   seize   tomato can

rolled   fortunate

Draw a picture or series of pictures illustrating the story.

COPYBOOK

My country, 'tis of thee,

Sweet land of liberty,

Of thee I sing;

Land where my fathers died,

Land of the Pilgrims' pride,

From every mountainside

Let freedom ring.

(Copy verses one below the other.)

My native country, thee,

Land of the noble free—

Thy name I love;

I love thy rocks and rills,

Thy woods and templed hills,

My heart with rapture thrills

Like that above.

Today is

_____
Day   Date   Year

PICTURE STUDY

_____

_____

_____

Dictation

_____

_____

_____

_____

_____

_____

_____

_____

Poem & Song Titles

Write the title of a poem or a song the same way you write the title of a chapter: capitalize the first word and every important word and enclose the title in quotes.

"America the Beautiful" by Katherine Lee Bates

Write a sentence about the song (poem) from which this week's copybook selection is taken. Use the correct form for writing a song title. Mention the name of the poet in your sentence.

_____

_____

_____

from MY COUNTRY, 'TIS OF THEE

Let music swell the breeze,

And ring from all the trees

Sweet freedom's song;

Let mortal tongues awake,

Let all that breathe partake,

Let rocks their silence break—

The sound prolong.

Our fathers' God, to Thee,

Author of liberty,

To Thee we sing;

Long may our land be bright

With freedom's holy light;

Protect us by Thy might,

Great God, our King.

~ Samuel Francis Smith

Today is _____

READ AND NARRATE _____

Reddy Fox Grows Curious

~ *The Adventures of Danny Meadow Mouse* by Thornton W. Burgess

Vocabulary to study before you read:

refuge	circling	pounce
curiosity	pursuit	swoop
understood	snarled	

Draw a picture or series of pictures illustrating the story.

COPYBOOK

Let music swell the breeze,

And ring from all the trees

    Sweet freedom's song;

Let mortal tongues awake,

Let all that breathe partake,

Let rocks their silence break—

    The sound prolong.

RHYMING WORDS

Write three words that rhyme with **breeze.**

Write three words that rhyme with **pride.**

Today is _____
               Day   Date   Year

Nature Study

Choose an insect and talk about its characteristics, covering the points below. Sketch the insect in the frame. Write the name of the insect on the line below the frame.

- ❑ Its size
- ❑ Its life cycle
- ❑ Its food
- ❑ Its means of protecting itself
- ❑ Its habits

Copybook

Our fathers' God, to Thee,

Author of liberty,

To Thee we sing;

Long may our land be bright

With freedom's holy light;

Protect us by Thy might,

Great God, our King.

_____

_____

_____

_____

_____

Possessive Forms

Find three possessive forms in today's copybook selection and write them below along with the thing possessed.

_____

_____

_____

Today is _____

                      Day   *Date*   *Year*

READ AND NARRATE

Reddy Fox Loses His Temper
~ The Adventures of Danny Meadow Mouse by Thornton W. Burgess

Vocabulary to study before you read:

torment	grinned	bully
victim	taunted	clever
learned	thrust	promptly
yelped	narrowest	rein

Draw a picture or series of pictures illustrating the story.

COPYBOOK

Let music swell the breeze,

And ring from all the trees

    Sweet freedom's song;

Let mortal tongues awake,

Let all that breathe partake,

Let rocks their silence break—

    The sound prolong.

(Copy verses one below the other.)

Our fathers' God to Thee,

Author of liberty,

    To Thee we sing;

Long may our land be bright

With freedom's holy light;

Protect us by Thy might,

    Great God, our King.

WEEK 12 ♦ DAY 4

Today is

_____

Day   Date   Year

PICTURE STUDY _____

_____

_____

_____

DICTATION

_____

_____

_____

_____

_____

_____

_____

ANTONYMS

Write at least one antonym for each word.

free   _____

all   _____

awake   _____

silence   _____

long   _____

bright   _____

light   _____

APPENDIX

Date:

Date:

Date:

Date:

Date:

Date:

Date:

Date:

Date:

DRAWING PAGE

Made in the USA
Monee, IL
21 August 2020